MW01671502

GOD'S PRO

Heart WITH Gratitude

JOYCE MEYER MINISTRIES

God's Promises That Fill Your Heart With Gratitude
Copyright © 2020 by Joyce Meyer Ministries

Published by Joyce Meyer Ministries, P.O. Box 655, Fenton, MO 63026
Printed in the United States of America.
ISBN: 978-1-951225-12-4

All rights reserved. No part of this publication may be reproduced, stored in a retrieval system, or transmitted in any form or by any means—including, but not limited, to being photocopied, recorded, or electronically stored or transmitted—without the prior written permission of the publisher.

Portions of material contained in this book have previously been published by *Joyce Meyer Ministries* and remain under copyright.

Scripture quotations marked (AMP) are taken from the Amplified® Bible, Copyright © 2015 by The Lockman Foundation. Used by permission.

Scripture quotations marked (AMPC) are taken from the Amplified Bible Classic Edition, Old Testament, copyright ©1965, 1987 by The Zondervan Corporation. The Amplified New Testament Classic, Edition, copyright © 1954, 1958, 1987 by The Lockman Foundation. Used by permission. All rights reserved.

Scripture quotations marked (NIV) are taken from the Holy Bible, New International Version®, NIV®. Copyright © 1973, 1978, 1984, 2011 by Biblica, Inc.™ Used by permission of Zondervan. All rights reserved worldwide. The "NIV" and "New International Version" are trademarks registered in the United States Patent and Trademark Office by Biblica, Inc.™

Scripture quotations marked (NKJV) are taken from the New King James Version®. Copyright © 1982 by Thomas Nelson. Used by permission. All rights reserved.

INTRODUCTION

I love the Word of God! It is amazing. It contains wisdom, encouragement, comfort and inspiration for every conceivable human problem or dilemma. **God's Word brings peace** and stability to our spirits, and it literally transforms our lives by renewing our minds.

I get excited to study God's Word every day, which is why I'm so glad you have this booklet full of Scripture promises. We've put it together as a tool for you to use in your journey to a better life that brings you closer to God. It is filled with scriptures about the importance of being grateful.

A life filled with **gratitude** for who God is and all He has done is a major key to having the life Jesus died to give you. And it's an attitude we have to cultivate on purpose because our natural tendency in challenging, or even just inconvenient circumstances, is to complain. While some people have a temperament that is more positive and appreciative than others, human nature, if it is not disciplined and controlled by the Holy Spirit, will often drift toward the negative. It seems we never have to try to complain, but it does take a determined decision, on purpose, to maintain a **grateful heart**.

Instead of complaining, let's choose to live each day with an attitude of gratitude. I'm not talking about just an occasional expression of thanks, but a continual lifestyle of thanksgiving. The person who lives consistently with this attitude is more peaceful, joyful and confident of **God's faithfulness**, and they expect God to work in their life day by day.

My hope is that the statements and scriptures in this book will inspire you to cultivate a **lifestyle of gratitude** as you gain deeper insights about the reasons you have to be grateful. And anytime you find negative thoughts filling your mind, use this booklet to help **refocus your thinking**.

As you discover how to be thankful in every situation, really believing that God is working everything out for your good, you will experience **God's goodness** every day that you live.

Grateful for you,
Dave & Joyce Meyer

A KEY TO BEING GRATEFUL

Just as the Bible instructs us to praise God and to worship Him, it also gives us reasons to thank Him and teaches us how to offer our gratitude to Him, as shown in the scriptures below:

- *We give praise and thanks to You, O God, we praise and give thanks; Your wondrous works declare that Your Name is near and they who invoke Your Name rehearse Your wonders.* **—Psalm 75:1 (AMPC)**

- *It is a good and delightful thing to give thanks to the Lord, to sing praises [with musical accompaniment] to Your name, O Most High . . .* **—Psalm 92:1 (AMPC)**

- *Let us come before His presence with thanksgiving; let us make a joyful noise to Him with songs of praise!* **—Psalm 95:2 (AMPC)**

Enter into His gates with thanksgiving and a thank offering and into His courts with praise! Be thankful and say so to Him, bless and affectionately praise His name! **—Psalm 100:4 (AMPC)**

Consistency is key to developing the habit of an attitude of gratitude. I want to suggest that you choose at least one of the statements and scriptures in this booklet each day and meditate on them throughout your day, asking God to show you how to apply His Word to your life.

As you practice being grateful, you'll find it gets easier to focus on God's promises and all that He has given you. As a result, you will also be much happier!

Each moment that we're given is a precious gift from God. We can choose to have a thankful attitude and live each moment full of joy . . . simply because God is good.

I am grateful for . . .

God's overwhelming love for me.

I will praise you, Lord, among the nations; I will sing of you among the peoples. For great is your love, higher than the heavens; your faithfulness reaches to the skies.

—Psalm 108:3–4 (NIV)

I am grateful for . . .

God's goodness.

Praise the Lord. Give thanks to the Lord, for he is good; his love endures forever. **—Psalm 106:1 (NIV)**

I am grateful for . . .

God's peace that calms my heart and mind.

"Peace I leave with you; My [perfect] peace I give to you; not as the world gives do I give to you. Do not let your heart be troubled, nor let it be afraid. [Let My perfect peace calm you in every circumstance and give you courage and strength for every challenge.]" **—John 14:27 (AMP)**

I am grateful for . . .

God's never-ending hope in my life.

May the God of your hope so fill you with all joy and peace in believing [through the experience of your faith] that by the power of the Holy Spirit you may abound and be overflowing (bubbling over) with hope. **—Romans 15:13 (AMPC)**

I am grateful for . . .

God's joy and gladness in my life.

Surely you have granted him unending blessings and made him glad with the joy of your presence. **—Psalm 21:6 (NIV)**

I am grateful for . . .

the many ways God meets all my needs.

And my God will meet all your needs according to the riches of his glory in Christ Jesus.

—Philippians 4:19 (NIV)

I am grateful for . . .

the incredible power of God.

. . . "Be still, and know that I am God; I will be exalted among the nations, I will be exalted in the earth."

—Psalm 46:10 (NIV)

I am grateful for . . .

God's plan for my life.

"For I know the plans I have for you," declares the Lord, "plans to prosper you and not to harm you, plans to give you hope and a future."

—Jeremiah 29:11 (NIV)

I am grateful for . . .

God's close, personal direction in my life.

"My sheep listen to my voice; I know them, and they follow me." **—John 10:27 (NIV)**

I am grateful for . . .

breakthrough and victory in my life.

But thanks be to God! He gives us the victory through our Lord Jesus Christ.

—1 Corinthians 15:57 (NIV)

I am grateful for . . .

the security of God's protection.

He who dwells in the shelter of the Most High will remain secure and rest in the shadow of the Almighty [whose power no enemy can withstand]. **—Psalm 91:1 (AMP)**

I am grateful for . . .

God's guidance.

Blessed are those who keep his statutes and seek him with all their heart—they do no wrong but follow his ways. **—Psalm 119:2–3 (NIV)**

I am grateful for . . .

God's rest.

"Come to me, all you who are weary and burdened and I will give you rest." **—Matthew 11:28 (NIV)**

I am grateful for . . .

the ability to hear, receive and obey God's voice.

Whether you turn to the right or to the left, your ears will hear a voice behind you, saying, "This is the way; walk in it." **—Isaiah 30:21 (NIV)**

I am grateful for . . .

God's faithfulness to lead me step by step each day.

The steps of a [good and righteous] man are directed and established by the Lord, and He delights in his way [and blesses his path]. When he falls, he will not be hurled down, because the Lord is the One who holds his hand and sustains him. **—Psalm 37:23–24 (AMP)**

I am grateful for . . .

freedom from my past.

It is for freedom that Christ has set us free. Stand firm, then, and do not let yourselves be burdened again by a yoke of slavery.

—Galatians 5:1 (NIV)

"When you are fiercely committed to God's purpose for your life, you will begin to experience all that He has for you."

—*Joyce*

I am grateful for . . .

God's trustworthy character.

Your kingdom is an everlasting kingdom, and your dominion endures through all generations. The Lord is trustworthy in all he promises and faithful in all he does.

—Psalm 145:13 (NIV)

I am grateful for . . .

God's mercy.

For the Lord is good; His mercy and lovingkindness are everlasting, His faithfulness [endures] to all generations. **—Psalm 100:5 (AMP)**

I am grateful for . . .

a sound mind.

For God has not given us a spirit of fear, but of power and of love and of a sound mind. **—2 Timothy 1:7 (NKJV)**

I am grateful for . . .

the good work God is doing in me every day.

I am convinced and confident of this very thing, that He who has begun a good work in you will [continue to] perfect and complete it until the day of Christ Jesus [the time of His return].
—Philippians 1:6 (AMP)

I am grateful for . . .

God's promises.

For no matter how many promises God has made, they are "Yes" in Christ. And so through him the "Amen" is spoken by us to the glory of God. —**2 Corinthians 1:20 (NIV)**

I am grateful for . . .

the opportunity to "do good" to others.

Therefore, as we have opportunity, let us do good to all people, especially to those who belong to the family of believers. **—Galatians 6:10 (NIV)**

I am grateful for . . .

the power to resist and overcome temptation.

No temptation has overtaken you except what is common to mankind. And God is faithful; he will not let you be tempted beyond what you can bear. But when you are tempted, he will also provide a way out so that you can endure it. **—1 Corinthians 10:13 (NIV)**

I am grateful for . . .

the hope I have in Christ that brings true joy to my life.

Command those who are rich in this present world not to be arrogant nor to put their hope in wealth, which is so uncertain, but to put their hope in God, who richly provides us with everything for our enjoyment. **—1 Timothy 6:17 (NIV)**

I am grateful for . . .

God's help every time I need Him.

So we take comfort and are encouraged and confidently say, "The Lord is my Helper [in time of need], I will not be afraid. What will man do to me?" **—Hebrews 13:6 (AMP)**

I am grateful for . . .

the assurance that God will guide, protect and bring fulfillment to my life.

After this, the word of the Lord came to Abram in a vision: "Do not be afraid, Abram. I am your shield, your very great reward."

—Genesis 15:1 (NIV)

I am grateful for . . .

the leading of the Holy Spirit.

"But the Helper (Comforter, Advocate, Intercessor—Counselor, Strengthener, Standby), the Holy Spirit, whom the Father will send in My name . . . He will teach you all things. And He will help you remember everything that I have told you." **—John 14:26 (AMP)**

I am grateful for . . .

the strength of the Lord.

The Lord is good, a strength and stronghold in the day of trouble; He knows [He recognizes, cares for, and understands fully] those who take refuge and trust in Him. **—Nahum 1:7 (AMP)**

I am grateful for . . .

the power in God's Word.

Blessed is the one . . . whose delight is in the law of the Lord, and who meditates on his law day and night. That person is like a tree planted by streams of water, which yields its fruit in season and whose leaf does not wither—whatever they do prospers. **—Psalm 1:1–3 (NIV)**

I am grateful for . . .

God's wisdom for my life.

For the Lord gives wisdom; from his mouth come knowledge and understanding. **—Proverbs 2:6 (NIV)**

I am grateful for . . .

the steadfast stability I have as I put my trust in God.

Those who trust in and rely on the Lord [with confident expectation] are like Mount Zion, which cannot be moved but remains forever. **—Psalm 125:1 (AMP)**

I am grateful for . . .

my health—spirit, soul and body.

Beloved, I pray that in every way you may succeed and prosper and be in good health [physically], just as [I know] your soul prospers [spiritually]. **—3 John 2 (AMP)**

"Trusting God allows us to enter His rest, and rest is a place of peace where we are able to enjoy our lives while being confident God is fighting our battles."

—Joyce

I am grateful for . . .

the purpose God has for my life.

Many are the plans in a person's heart, but it is the Lord's purpose that prevails. **—Proverbs 19:21 (NIV)**

I am grateful for . . .

the assurance that God wants me to give Him all of my cares, worries and concerns.

. . . Casting all your cares [all your anxieties, all your worries, and all your concerns, once and for all] on Him, for He cares about you [with deepest affection, and watches over you very carefully].

—1 Peter 5:7 (AMP)

I am grateful for . . .

God's plans and that He's created me to do great things in this world.

For we are His workmanship [His own master work, a work of art], created in Christ Jesus [reborn from above—spiritually transformed, renewed, ready to be used] for good works, which God prepared [for us] beforehand [taking paths which He set], so that we would walk in them [living the good life which He prearranged and made ready for us]. **—Ephesians 2:10 (AMP)**

I am grateful for . . .

the security I have as I follow the wisdom of God.

"But whoever listens to me (Wisdom) will live securely and in confident trust and will be at ease, without fear or dread of evil."

—Proverbs 1:33 (AMP)

I am grateful for . . .

the privilege to pray and talk with God.

"For everyone who keeps on asking receives, and he who keeps on seeking finds, and to him who keeps on knocking, it will be opened." **—Matthew 7:8 (AMP)**

I am grateful for . . .

the strength to be patient.

But let endurance and steadfastness and patience have full play and do a thorough work, so that you may be [people] perfectly and fully developed [with no defects], lacking in nothing.

—James 1:4 (AMPC)

I am grateful for . . .

the confidence I have in God to do whatever I need to do in life.

For you have been my hope, Sovereign Lord, my confidence since my youth. —**Psalm 71:5 (NIV)**

I am grateful for . . .

the ability to love God, myself and others.

. . . "'Love the Lord your God with all your heart and with all your soul and with all your strength and with all your mind'; and, 'Love your neighbor as yourself.'" **—Luke 10:27 (NIV)**

I am grateful for . . .

freedom from fear.

". . . Be strong and courageous. Do not be afraid; do not be discouraged, for the Lord your God will be with you wherever you go." **—Joshua 1:9 (NIV)**

I am grateful for . . .

God's abundant and amazing grace.

And God is able to make all grace [every favor and earthly blessing] come in abundance to you, so that you may always [under all circumstances, regardless of the need] have complete sufficiency in everything [being completely self-sufficient in Him], and have an abundance for every good work and act of charity. **—2 Corinthians 9:8 (AMP)**

I am grateful for . . .

freedom from worry.

"So do not worry, saying, 'What shall we eat?' or 'What shall we drink?' or 'What shall we wear?' For the pagans run after all these things, and your heavenly Father knows that you need them. But seek first his kingdom and his righteousness, and all these things will be given to you as well. Therefore do not worry about tomorrow, for tomorrow will worry about itself. Each day has enough trouble of its own." **—Matthew 6:31–34 (NIV)**

I am grateful for . . .

forgiveness that gives me a guilt-free life.

Therefore there is now no condemnation [no guilty verdict, no punishment) for those who are in Christ Jesus [who believe in Him as personal Lord and Savior]. **—Romans 8:1 (AMP)**

I am grateful for . . .

the love God shows me through my family and friends and the privilege I have to love them.

[Let your] love be sincere (a real thing); hate what is evil [loathe all ungodliness, turn in horror from wickedness], but hold fast to that which is good. Love one another with brotherly affection [as members of one family], giving precedence and showing honor to one another. **—Romans 12:9–10 (AMPC)**

I am grateful for . . .

my new life in Christ.

Therefore if anyone is in Christ . . . he is a new creature [reborn and renewed by the Holy Spirit]; the old things [the previous moral and spiritual condition] have passed away. Behold, new things have come. . . . **—2 Corinthians 5:17 (AMP)**

I am grateful for . . .

no more shame.

And hope does not put us to shame, because God's love has been poured out into our hearts through the Holy Spirit, who has been given to us. **—Romans 5:5 (NIV)**

I am grateful for . . .

my faith in God and my relationship with Him.

. . . Fixing our eyes on Jesus, the pioneer and perfecter of faith. . . . **—Hebrews 12:2 (NIV)**

"Give yourself and your worries to God, worship Him and begin enjoying the abundant life He has for you."

—*Joyce*

I am grateful for . . .

God's never-ending provision.

Praise the Lord, my soul . . . who satisfies your desires with good things so that your youth is renewed like the eagle's.
—Psalm 103:1, 5 (NIV)

I am grateful for . . .

healing in my body.

But he was pierced for our transgressions, he was crushed for our iniquities; the punishment that brought us peace was on him, and by his wounds we are healed. **—Isaiah 53:5 (NIV)**

I am grateful for . . .

today.

This [day in which God has saved me] is the day which the Lord has made; let us rejoice and be glad in it.

—Psalm 118:24 (AMP)

I am grateful for . . .

God's grace, mercy and unselfish love for me.

Let your gentle spirit [your graciousness, unselfishness, mercy, tolerance, and patience] be known to all people. The Lord is near.

—Philippians 4:5 (AMP)

I am grateful for . . .

the forgiveness of my sins and God's promise to restore my life.

"If my people, who are called by my name, will humble themselves and pray and seek my face and turn from their wicked ways, then I will hear from heaven, and I will forgive their sin and will heal their land."

—2 Chronicles 7:14 (NIV)

I am grateful for . . .

the mind of Christ.

For who has known the mind and purposes of the Lord, so as to instruct Him? But we have the mind of Christ [to be guided by His thoughts and purposes]. **—1 Corinthians 2:16 (AMP)**

I am grateful for . . .

the Lord's wise counsel in my life.

I will praise the Lord, who counsels me; even at night my heart instructs me. I keep my eyes always on the Lord. With him at my right hand, I will not be shaken.

—Psalm 16:7–8 (NIV)

I am grateful for . . .

God's everlasting love and kindness.

. . . "I have loved you with an everlasting love;
I have drawn you with unfailing kindness."

—Jeremiah 31:3 (NIV)

I am grateful for . . .

the joy of the Lord, which gives me strength.

". . . The joy of the Lord is your strength." **—Nehemiah 8:10 (NIV)**

I am grateful for . . .

shelter from the storm.

God is our refuge and strength, an ever-present help in trouble. **—Psalm 46:1 (NIV)**

I am grateful for . . .

victory as God fights my battles.

"'You will not have to fight this battle. Take up your positions; stand firm and see the deliverance the Lord will give you . . . Do not be afraid; do not be discouraged. Go out to face them tomorrow, and the Lord will be with you.'" **—2 Chronicles 20:17 (NIV)**

I am grateful for . . .

the passion to love others like Jesus.

Jesus replied: "'Love the Lord your God with all your heart and with all your soul and with all your mind.' This is the first and greatest commandment. And the second is like it: 'Love your neighbor as yourself.'" **—Matthew 22:37–39 (NIV)**

I am grateful for . . .

the provision, peace, fulfillment and guidance I have from God as my Good Shepherd.

The Lord is my shepherd, I lack nothing. He makes me lie down in green pastures, he leads me beside quiet waters, he refreshes my soul. He guides me along the right paths for his name's sake. **—Psalm 23:1–3 (NIV)**

I am grateful for . . .

my authority as a follower of Jesus.

"I have given you authority to trample on snakes and scorpions and to overcome all the power of the enemy; nothing will harm you." **—Luke 10:19 (NIV)**

I am grateful for . . .

the total confidence I have that God hears and answers my prayers according to His plans for my life.

This is the confidence we have in approaching God: that if we ask anything according to his will, he hears us. And if we know that he hears us—whatever we ask—we know that we have what we have asked of him. **—1 John 5:14–15 (NIV)**

I am grateful for . . .

the assurance I have that God is always bigger than my problems.

. . . For everyone born of God overcomes the world. This is the victory that has overcome the world, even our faith. **—1 John 5:4 (NIV)**

"God has a personalized plan for each of us, a plan that will lead us to victory."

—*Joyce*

I am grateful for . . .

God's faithfulness to meet my needs as I seek Him and put my trust in Him.

. . . They who seek (inquire of and require) the Lord [by right of their need and on the authority of His Word], none of them shall lack any beneficial thing.

—Psalm 34:10 (AMPC)

I am grateful for . . .

the love of God that shines brightly in me and points others to Jesus.

"In the same way, let your light shine before others, that they may see your good deeds and glorify your Father in heaven." **—Matthew 5:16 (NIV)**

I am grateful for . . .

Jesus, who is greater than my enemy and gives me everything I need to overcome the enemy's attacks in this world.

You, dear children, are from God and have overcome them, because the one who is in you is greater than the one who is in the world. **—1 John 4:4 (NIV)**

I am grateful for . . .

God's mercies, which are new every day for me.

It is because of the Lord's mercy and loving-kindness that we are not consumed, because His [tender] compassions fail not. They are new every morning; great and abundant is Your stability and faithfulness. **—Lamentations 3:22–23 (AMPC)**

I am grateful for . . .

Jesus, who gave His life so my sins could be forgiven.

". . . For this is My blood of the [new and better] covenant, which [ratifies the agreement and] is being poured out for many [as a substitutionary atonement] for the forgiveness of sins." **—Matthew 26:28 (AMP)**

I am grateful for . . .

the ability to forgive others the same way Jesus has forgiven me.

Then Peter came to Jesus and asked, "Lord, how many times shall I forgive my brother or sister who sins against me? Up to seven times?" Jesus answered, "I tell you, not seven times, but seventy times seven." **—Matthew 18:21–22 (NIV)**

I am grateful for . . .

God's complete and total forgiveness of my sin.

. . . "Their sins and lawless acts I will remember no more."

—Hebrews 10:17 (NIV)

I am grateful for . . .

Jesus' promise to heal my broken heart.

He heals the brokenhearted and binds up their wounds [healing their pain and comforting their sorrow]. **—Psalm 147:3 (AMP)**

I am grateful for . . .

the gift of being made right with God.

God made him who had no sin to be sin for us, so that in him we might become the righteousness of God.

—2 Corinthians 5:21 (NIV)

I am grateful for . . .

God's Word that lights my way.

Your word is a lamp for my feet, a light on my path. **—Psalm 119:10 5 (NIV)**

I am grateful for . . .

every good gift from God.

Every good and perfect gift is from above, coming down from the Father of the heavenly lights, who does not change like shifting shadows. **—James 1:17 (NIV)**

I am grateful for . . .

God's tender loving care for me.

"Look at the birds of the air; they do not sow or reap or store away in barns, and yet your heavenly Father feeds them. Are you not much more valuable than they?" **—Matthew 6:26 (NIV)**

I am grateful for . . .

the freedom from sin and a place in God's family.

Jesus replied, "Very truly I tell you, everyone who sins is a slave to sin. Now a slave has no permanent place in the family, but a son belongs to it forever. So if the Son sets you free, you will be free indeed." **—John 8:34–36 (NIV)**

I am grateful for . . .

God helping me to be an example of His love to others.

But thanks be to God, who always leads us in triumph in Christ, and through us spreads and makes evident everywhere the sweet fragrance of the knowledge of Him. **—2 Corinthians 2:14 (AMP)**

I am grateful for . . .

God's grace and His power that works in me when I am weak.

But he said to me, "My grace is sufficient for you, for my power is made perfect in weakness." Therefore I will boast all the more gladly about my weaknesses, so that Christ's power may rest on me. **—2 Corinthians 12:9 (NIV)**

I am grateful for . . .

the sacrifice Jesus made so I can have new life in Him.

I have been crucified with Christ and I no longer live, but Christ lives in me. The life I now live in the body, I live by faith in the Son of God, who loved me and gave himself for me. **—Galatians 2:20 (NIV)**

"Of all the things that we have to be grateful for in our lives, love is at the top of the list. Loving and being loved bring purpose and meaning to life. The world is looking for love, but they are really looking for God because God is love."

—Joyce

I am grateful for . . .

God's Word bringing joy and life to me and those around me.

Let the message of Christ dwell among you richly as you teach and admonish one another with all wisdom through psalms, hymns, and songs from the Spirit, singing to God with gratitude in your hearts. **—Colossians 3:16 (NIV)**

I am grateful for . . .

God's Word that works in my life to reveal my sin and transform me to be more like Christ.

For the word of God is alive and active. Sharper than any double-edged sword, it penetrates even to dividing soul and spirit, joints and marrow; it judges the thoughts and attitudes of the heart.

—Hebrews 4:12 (NIV)

I am grateful for . . .

the love of God that enables me to love others as Jesus loves me.

. . . And walk continually in love [that is, value one another—practice empathy and compassion, unselfishly seeking the best for others], just as Christ also loved you and gave Himself up for us, an offering and sacrifice to God [slain for you, so that it became] a sweet fragrance.

—Ephesians 5:2 (AMP)

I am grateful for . . .

the opportunities God gives me to overcome evil with good.

. . . "If your enemy is hungry, feed him; if he is thirsty, give him something to drink. . . ." Do not be overcome by evil, but overcome evil with good.

—Romans 12:20–21 (NIV)

I am grateful for . . .

God's amazing love and generosity and His desire to take care of me.

He who did not spare his own Son, but gave him up for us all—how will he not also, along with him, graciously give us all things? **—Romans 8:32 (NIV)**

I am grateful for . . .

the truth of God's Word that sets me free.

. . . Jesus said, "If you hold to my teaching, you are really my disciples. Then you will know the truth, and the truth will set you free." **—John 8:31–32 (NIV)**

I am grateful for . . .

freedom from the law of sin and death.

For the law of the Spirit of life [which is] in Christ Jesus [the law of our new being] has set you free from the law of sin and of death. **—Romans 8:2 (AMP)**

I am grateful for . . .

the gift of the Holy Spirit.

What we have received is not the spirit of the world, but the Spirit who is from God, so that we may understand what God has freely given us.

—1 Corinthians 2:12 (NIV)

I am grateful for . . .

the ability to do the will of God.

Now may the God of peace, who through the blood of the eternal covenant brought back from the dead our Lord Jesus, that great Shepherd of the sheep, equip you with everything good for doing his will, and may he work in us what is pleasing to him, through Jesus Christ, to whom be glory for ever and ever. Amen. **—Hebrews 13:20–21 (NIV)**

I am grateful for . . .

the hope—the confident expectation of good things—that comes from the Lord.

"And now, Lord, for what do I expectantly wait? My hope [my confident expectation] is in You."

—Psalm 39:7 (AMP)

I am grateful for . . .

the life of God that brings healing and restoration to my body.

And if the Spirit of him who raised Jesus from the dead is living in you, he who raised Christ from the dead will also give life to your mortal bodies because of his Spirit who lives in you. **—Romans 8:11 (NIV)**

I am grateful for . . .

the peace of Christ when I'm faced with trouble in this world.

"I have told you these things, so that in me you may have peace. In this world you will have trouble. But take heart! I have overcome the world." **—John 16:33 (NIV)**

I am grateful for . . .

God's grace and righteousness at work in my life because of what Jesus has done for me.

For if, by the trespass of the one man, death reigned through that one man, how much more will those who receive God's abundant provision of grace and of the gift of righteousness reign in life through the one man, Jesus Christ! **—Romans 5:17 (NIV)**

I am grateful for . . .

the peace of God that brings clarity in the midst of confusion.

For God . . . is not a God of confusion and disorder but of peace and order. . . .

—1 Corinthians 14:33 (AMP)

I am grateful for . . .

God's amazing favor in my life.

For You, O Lord, bless the righteous man [the one who is in right standing with You]; You surround him with favor as with a shield. **—Psalm 5:12 (AMP)**

I am grateful for . . .

freedom to press on each day in God's plan for my life.

. . . But one thing I do: Forgetting what is behind and straining toward what is ahead, I press on toward the goal to win the prize for which God has called me heavenward in Christ Jesus.

—Philippians 3:13–14 (NIV)

"Peace is one of the greatest blessings that God has given us, and we should thank Him for it daily. Simply desiring a life of peace is not enough. You have to pursue peace with God, peace with yourself and peace with those around you."

—Joyce

I am grateful for . . .

the help God gives me to become more like Him.

. . . So that you may live a life worthy of the Lord and please him in every way: bearing fruit in every good work, growing in the knowledge of God, being strengthened with all power according to his glorious might so that you may have great endurance and patience, and giving joyful thanks to the Father. . . . **—Colossians 1:10–12 (NIV)**

I am grateful for . . .

the spiritual armor of God that continually equips me to overcome the enemy.

Therefore put on the full armor of God, so that when the day of evil comes, you may be able to stand your ground, and after you have done everything, to stand. . . . Take up the shield of faith, with which you can extinguish all the flaming arrows of the evil one. **—Ephesians 6:13–16 (NIV)**

I am grateful for . . .

God's amazing peace that gives me freedom from worry, anxiety and fearful thoughts.

Do not be anxious about anything, but in every situation, by prayer and petition, with thanksgiving, present your requests to God. And the peace of God, which transcends all understanding, will guard your hearts and your minds in Christ Jesus. **—Philippians 4:6–7 (NIV)**

I am grateful for . . .

the power in God's Word to renew my mind so I can understand what is good and acceptable in His sight.

Do not conform to the pattern of this world, but be transformed by the renewing of your mind. Then you will be able to test and approve what God's will is—his good, pleasing and perfect will.

—Romans 12:2 (NIV)

I am grateful for . . .

God's wisdom and direction in every area of my life.

Trust in the Lord with all your heart and lean not on your own understanding; in all your ways submit to him, and he will make your paths straight. **—Proverbs 3:5–6 (NIV)**

I am grateful for . . .

God as my Creator and Shepherd and that I belong to Him.

Know and fully recognize with gratitude that the Lord Himself is God; it is He who has made us, not we ourselves [and we are His]. We are His people and the sheep of His pasture.

—Psalm 100:3 (AMP)

"The person who has developed an *attitude of gratitude* is one who is thankful and grateful for every single thing that God is doing in his or her life day by day."

—Joyce

Prayer of Thanksgiving

Father, I am so thankful for the promises and wisdom that I find in Your Word. Today, I choose to live a thankful life because You are awesome and I am truly grateful for the life I have in Christ, my Lord and Savior. Thank You for showing me who You are and how You want to be involved in every area and circumstance of my life. I love You, Lord! Thank You for loving me!

Do you have a real relationship with Jesus?

God loves you! He created you to be a special, unique, one-of-a-kind individual, and He has a specific purpose and plan for your life. And through a personal relationship with your Creator—God—you can discover a way of life that will truly satisfy your soul.

No matter who you are, what you've done or where you are in your life right now, **God's love and grace are greater than your sin**—your mistakes. Jesus willingly gave His life so you can receive forgiveness from God and have new life in Him. He's just waiting for you to invite Him to be your Savior and Lord.

If you are ready to commit your life to Jesus and follow Him, all you have to do is ask Him to forgive you for your sins and give you a fresh start in the life you are meant to live. **Begin by praying this prayer . . .**

Lord Jesus, thank You for giving Your life for me and forgiving me of my sins so I can have a personal relationship with You. I am sincerely sorry for the mistakes I've made, and I know I need You to help me live right.

Your Word says in Romans 10:9, "If you declare with your mouth, 'Jesus is Lord,' and believe in your heart that God raised him from the dead, you will be saved" (NIV). I believe You are the Son of God and confess You as my Savior and Lord. Take me just as I am, and work in my heart, making me the person You want me to be. I want to live for You, Jesus, and I am so grateful that You are giving me a fresh start in my new life with You today.

I love You, Jesus!

It's so amazing to know that God loves us so much! He wants to have a deep, intimate relationship with us that grows every day as we spend time with Him in prayer and Bible study. And we want to encourage you in your new life in Christ.

Please visit **joycemeyer.org/KnowJesus** to request Joyce's book ***A New Way of Living***, which is our gift to you. We also have other free resources online to help you take your next steps in pursuing everything God has for you.

Congratulations on your fresh start in your life in Christ! We are so excited for you and can't wait to hear from you!

Joyce Meyer
Ministries®

Sharing Christ – Loving People

Joyce Meyer Ministries is called to share the Gospel and extend the love of Christ. Through media, we teach people how to apply biblical truth to every aspect of their lives and encourage God's people to serve the world around them. Through our missions arm, *Hand of Hope*, we provide global humanitarian aid, feed the hungry, clothe the poor, minister to the elderly, widows and orphans, visit prisoners and reach out to people of all ages and in all walks of life. *Joyce Meyer Ministries* is built on a foundation of faith, integrity and dedicated supporters who share this call.

For more information about *Joyce Meyer Ministries*, please visit www.joycemeyer.org or call (800) 727-9673. Outside the U.S. call (636) 349-0303.

Joyce Meyer Ministries • P.O. Box 655 • Fenton, MO 63026 • joycemeyer.org